CW00543988

EUSEBIUS

EUSEBIUS

THE FIRST CHRISTIAN HISTORIAN

Edited by
Robert Van de Weyer

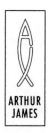

Published in 1996 by Arthur James Ltd.
4 Broadway Road, Evesham, Worcestershire, WR11 6BH

ISBN 0-85305-342-1

Text © 1996 Robert Van de Weyer
All rights reserved by Arthur James Ltd.

Typeset by Little Gidding Books in Bembo.
Printed and bound in Great Britain by Biddles Ltd, Guildford.

PREFACE

The original community at Little Gidding was founded in 1626 by Nicholas Ferrar; their beautiful chapel continues to attract numerous visitors. A new community formed in the late 1970s; and, like its predecessor, it includes families and single people, following a simple rule and pattern of prayer.

Little Gidding Books is the publishing arm of the community. In addition to its Prayer Book it publishes each quarter a book of daily readings, and each year a set of readings and meditations for the festival weeks and Lent. These sets of readings may be used in conjunction with the Prayer Book, or on their own. They are supplied directly to Friends of Little Gidding, and are also available to the wider public through bookshops.

The community is dedicated to Christ the Sower; hence its symbol is a cross made from ears of corn. The hand in which 'Little Gidding Books' is written on the cover is that of Nicholas Ferrar – the words have been taken from his letters.

If you would like to have more information, please write to:

The Community of Christ the Sower
Little Gidding
Huntingdon
PE17 5RJ
United Kingdom

INTRODUCTION

If Eusebius had not written his *History of the Church*, we would know very little about the first three centuries of Christianity, from the age of the apostles through to the accession of the first Christian emperor. From Eusebius we learn about the terrible persecutions and the courage of the martyrs; about obscure doctrinal disputes and personality clashes that split congregations; and about the acts of charity performed by ordinary church members which so impressed many of their pagan neighbours – and which were the main reason for the astonishing growth of the church in this period. His work has all the marks of historical accuracy: he quotes documents at length; he compiles lists of bishops; when he refers to a theologian he gives a bibliography of his works; and he is constantly alluding to the sources of his information. Thus we feel we can trust him. And amidst this scholarly material, he loves to tell stories which both grip the reader's attention, and cast light on the inner spiritual reality of events.

He was born in about 260, probably in Caesarea, the city built by Herod the Great on the coast of Palestine. As a young man he became a disciple and friend of Pamphilus, who established in Caesarea a school of theology, with a large library. For the following two decades he worked closely with Pamphilus on various theological projects, including the exposition of parts of the New Testament. Then in the great persecution ordered by Emperor Diocletian in 303 Pamphilus was arrested; and soon afterwards Eusebius was imprisoned as well. Happily they shared a cell, and continued their theological labours. But in 309 Pamphilus was subjected to a series of severe tortures, in the hope that he would publicly renounce his faith. He remained constant, and was executed a year later. Eusebius escaped a similar fate, and was later accused of having made some act of submission to appease his captors – a charge he hotly denied.

When Constantine became emperor in 312, Eusebius, like many Christians, saw his enthronement as the climax of a grand divine plan. As Eusebius constantly emphasizes in his *History*, Christians were loyal and law-abiding citizens, who wished to uphold imperial rule; their only crime was that they could not worship the emperor as a god. Thus Eusebius saw the Roman Empire as divinely ordained, both to bring peace to its subjects, and to provide an earthly framework within which the gospel could spread and the church grow. While he abhorred the persecutions, Eusebius saw them in retrospect as God's means of refining and purifying his church. And when Constantine declared Christianity as the favoured religion of the empire, even granting state funds for building places of worship, Eusebius concluded that the church was now ready to assume this central role.

Sadly, however, the doctrinal disputes, which had divided Christians even amidst persecution, now erupted with re-newed vigour; and within a few months Constantine was writing to bishops throughout the empire to complain of their quarrelsome behaviour. Eusebius became bishop of his native city in 314, but was himself soon under suspicion of heresy. The main focus of debate was the relationship between the human and divine aspects of Christ's nature. Eusebius' inclina-tion was to emphasize the humanity of Christ, presenting him as a figure with whom ordinary people could identify. Others, however, wanted to stress his divinity, and thus to assert his unique authority; they went on to argue that this made the church, as Christ's body on earth, the sole vehicle of salvation. Judging by his early proclamations Constantine preferred Eusebius' view; indeed, while he personally preferred the Christian religion, he recognized the validity of other faiths, and ordered that everyone should be free to worship 'according to his own inclination and wish'. But as the dispute raged with ever greater ferocity, he began to fear for the safety of the empire. So, after various less drastic attempts to bring peace, in 325 he called every church leader from throughout the empire to a council, at which he would preside.

The Council of Nicaea was the climax of Eusebius' ecclesiastical career. For much of the proceedings he sat at the Emperor's side, interpreting the arcane theological points to him. And he himself wrote a creed which at one stage found favour with both sides. The eventual creed gave greater weight than Eusebius wished to the divinity of Christ and his spiritual equality with the Father; but for the sake of unity he put his name to it, which allowed the Emperor to declare it as definitive. Eusebius, who was by now an old man, retired to Caesarea, rejecting all offers of promotion to more prestigious bishoprics. He strenuously sought to impose the Nicene formula on the congregations of Palestine, and even expelled priests who refused to conform. But he devoted the bulk of his remaining years to his first love, theological scholarship. He died in 340, three years after his beloved Emperor; and his final work was a biography of Constantine.

Eusebius was not a great writer. His *History* is poorly constructed: it is more a jumble of disconnected pieces, than a narrative; and there is little reflection or insight. But it is an astonishing feat of research. To compile it he visited libraries throughout the Christian world, reading dusty scrolls and copying relevant passages; indeed most of the works he quotes have been lost in their original form, so his extracts are all that remain. Much of the material, especially the lists and bibliographies, is dull to all except fellow scholars. But his prose begins to sparkle as he describes specific events and people. In fact his real genius is as a storyteller; and the stories he tells are our windows onto the life and times of the early church. These stories make up the present abridged edition of his *History*.

Robert Van de Weyer

1

As early as the first century of the Christian era, there were men and women who felt prompted by God to renounce all their property, handing it over to the poor, and then to go and live in remote parts of the countryside. They built themselves tiny huts, and ate wild fruits and roots which they collected from the forests. They spent many hours of each day and night in silent meditation, and in praying for the needs of the world. Sometimes they constructed small chapels: and each week groups of these people would gather to worship God together. They also studied the scriptures in great depth, in order to discern the meaning of every sentence and every word. They became known as doctors of the soul. This is because people from the cities went out to see them, asking their advice on every kind of matter. The doctors listened carefully to them, discerning the inner moral diseases that lay behind each problem. They then offered advice as to how the moral diseases could be cured. In this way numerous people, having seen these doctors of the soul, were able to follow the way of Christ with perfect sincerity and purity of heart. These doctors of the soul also composed many beautiful hymns and songs praising God which they taught to those who visited them.

Towards the end of his life John the apostle went to live in Ephesus. From there he used to travel to the Christian communities in the surrounding districts, appointing pastors, encouraging the people, and settling disputes. One day he arrived at a certain place where he had appointed a pastor some time earlier. While he was there he met a young man who was exceptionally handsome and strong. John spoke to the young man about the gospel of Christ, and the young man responded with great ardour of spirit. So John took him to the pastor, saying: 'I entrust this young man to your keeping. Under your guidance may he grow in the faith and the love of Christ.' When John had left, the pastor took the young man into his home, treating him like his own son. After some months he gave him baptism, which he declared to be the seal of faith. The pastor now allowed the young man much greater freedom. But unfortunately the young man was not yet mature enough in the Spirit to use this freedom wisely, and he was led astray by others of his own age who were idle and dissolute. First they took him to expensive entertainment, making him pay with his own money. Then, when his money had run out, they took him out at night and showed him how to rob money and jewellery from people's homes. Like a powerful hard-mouthed horse, he took the bit between his teeth, galloping off the straight road and down a precipice. He directed his youthful vitality to evil, just as earlier he had directed it to righteousness.

3

After some time John returned to the place where he had met the handsome young man. He said to the pastor: 'Come now, pay me back the deposit which in Christ's name I left in your keeping.' At first the pastor was taken aback, thinking that he was being asked for money which he had never received. John saw his confusion and added: 'It is the young man I am asking for.' The pastor sighed and started to weep. 'The young man is dead,' he said. 'How did he die?' John asked. 'I mean he is dead to the world,' the pastor said, and related what had occurred. John immediately went off to the place in the hills where the young man and his evil friends were living. When he arrived the men seized him. John made no attempt to escape and asked no mercy. 'I demand to see the young man whom you have led astray,' John cried out. The young man heard the commotion and came to see what was happening. As soon as the young man saw John, he was filled with shame, and he started to run away. With a sudden burst of strength John broke free of his captors, and, forgetting his age, ran after the young man. As he ran, John shouted out: 'Why do you run away from me, my child? I am your father; I am old and frail. Be sorry for me, not frightened of me. You still have your whole life ahead of you. Soon I shall die, and I will intercede for you with Christ.'

4

The young man, who had lapsed into evil ways, heard the apostle John begging him to stop. As John referred to himself as the young man's father, tears welled up in his youthful eyes, and his legs began to tremble. Finally his legs could run no further, and he fell to the ground. John caught up with him, panting at the exertion of running so far. As soon as he had regained his breath, John knelt down and clasped the young man to his bosom. At first John could not speak, but only weep; and he baptized the young man a second time with his tears. The young man also wept, and John knew that those were tears of repentance. John took the young man's right hand into his own, and placed it over his heart. 'I solemnly pledge', John said, 'that I will not rest until I have gained pardon for this young man from the Saviour himself.' John then let go the young man, and began to pray. After a few short minutes John smiled broadly, knowing that Christ had gladly forgiven the young man, and was ready to welcome him back into his fold. So John led the young man back to the town. And there the pastor who had baptized the young man welcomed him with open arms.

5

Late in the first century a sect arose, calling itself Christian, led by a man called Cerinthus. He claimed to have had visions directly from Jesus Christ himself. And in these visions, so he said, Jesus told him that he did not rise from the dead in body, but in spirit only. Cerinthus concluded from these visions that the human body is essentially corrupt, and that the human spirit can only be saved by breaking free from the body. So Cerinthus taught his followers to show their contempt for the body by indulging all their lusts and desires. Great banquets were held where wine was drunk in great profusion, and men and women used one another's bodies to gratify themselves. The apostle John heard about this terrible sect, and ordered his companions not even to speak to Cerinthus and his followers. 'Do not imagine that in your own strength you are strong enough to resist Cerinthus and his evil teaching,' John said. John applied the same warning to himself. One day, when he want to the bathhouse to wash himself, he found Cerinthus inside. Instantly John turned on his heels and ran away. But mercifully the sect destroyed itself. Amidst the other lusts and desires which grew and flourished in the bosom of Cerinthus and his followers, the lust for violence took root. Thus in mutual anger and hatred they attacked one another, until only a few were left.

6

A man called Nicolaus had a very attractive young wife, to whom he was devoted. But when he became a Christian, Nicolaus misunderstood the teachings of the gospel about sexual matters. From the moment of his conversion Nicolaus gave up all sexual relations with his wife. His wife had already borne him a son and three daughters; and as they grew up Nicolaus forbade them from marrying, telling them that the gospel required them to treat all physical desire with contempt. Others were so impressed by Nicolaus that they followed his example, forming a sect which became known as the Nicolaitans; it is mentioned in the Revelation of John. No one disputes the sincerity of Nicolaus, and everyone respects the strength of his desire to be a slave to God, rather than a slave to pleasure. But Jesus does not require all his followers to be celibate. The apostles Peter and Philip had families, and Philip gave his daughters in marriage. Paul refers to his 'yoke-fellow' – although he did not take her with him on his journeys, for fear of hindering his ministry. Thus we can conclude that all Christians, even the apostles themselves, are free to marry and to have sexual relations, according to God's will.

It is shameful to record that during the persecution instigated by the wicked Emperor Nero, those who reported Christians to the authorities were not generally pagans, but other Christians. These other Christians, who proved to be traitors, held doctrines which distorted the pure teachings of the gospel; and in order to promote their twisted doctrines, they wished to see true, faithful Christians put to death. One notable victim of such treachery was Symeon, the second bishop of Jerusalem. Symeon was already a very old man when a group of treacherous Christians went to Atticus, the governor, and told him how the venerable Bishop was winning many converts. So Atticus sent soldiers to arrest Symeon. For many days the most cruel tortures were inflicted on his frail body. But his spirit remained utterly indifferent to bodily pain; so while his body writhed in agony, hymns of praise poured from his lips. Finally the torturers despaired of forcing him to renounce his faith. So Atticus ordered him to be crucified. Symeon was overjoyed to share the same fate as the Lord. Sadly I must record that similar treachery occurred in many subsequent persecutions; so we must conclude that the greatest enemies of Christ are not pagans, but Christians whose faith has become twisted.

8

Pliny the Younger, when he became governor of Bithynia, was at first diligent in hunting down Christians. But he soon became alarmed at the number of Christians, both in his own province and elsewhere; and he quaked at the prospect of executing countless thousands of men and women who were doing no harm to the social order. Indeed he recognized that faithful Christians were invariably upright and law-abiding citizens. Thus he wrote to Emperor Trajan, to tell him that Christians were doing nothing improper or illegal; their only unusual activity was to rise at dawn and sing praises to Christ. He added that they conformed to the law in every respect, repudiating adultery, fraud, and any other possible crime. Trajan therefore issued a decree, ordering that members of the Christian community were no longer to be hunted, and that they should be arrested and punished only if they openly propagated their beliefs. The result was that in many places the threat of persecution was lifted. But in other places those who wished to inflict harm on Christians could still find many pretexts for arresting them; so sporadic attacks continued to blaze up in one province or another.

Ignatius, the second bishop of Antioch, was arrested for his beliefs, and taken from Syria to Rome; there he was put into the arena and eaten by wild beasts, for the entertainment of the people. During his journey to Rome he was guarded by ten soldiers who regularly beat him; and if he showed kindness to them, they beat him more severely. But despite the pain and discomfort, each evening he wrote a letter to the local church, encouraging the Christians in their faith and urging them to be on their guard against false teachers. In these letters he frequently referred to his coming martyrdom, asking them to pray that the animals would devour him quickly. The people acknowledged Ignatius as a hero of the faith, but he himself remained humble. In one letter he wrote that only with the prospect of imminent death did he become certain of the resurrection of Christ; this in turn convinced him that he would rise again with Christ. In his final letter he referred to himself as God's wheat, to be ground by the teeth of beasts, in order to become pure bread. When he entered the arena in Rome the animals at first refused to attack him, as if they sensed his sanctity; but to the amazement of the crowd he coaxed them towards him.

Early in the second century one of the most eminent
evangelists was a man called Quadratus. His heart was on fire
with a passion for truth, and with a desire to spread the truth
across the world. In order to become an evangelist, he decided
that he must first renounce all worldly responsibilities and
possessions. So he sold all his belongings, and distributed the
money he received amongst the poor. Then he began to travel
from place to place, preaching the good news wherever he
went. He also requested those skilled in writing to copy out
the gospels and epistles, and he carried these to the places he
visited. In most places he was successful, founding a new
Christian community. He would then stay for a few months,
choosing men with the ability to become pastors, and passing
on to them in detail the teachings of Christ. Once he was
satisfied that these pastors could guide the new flock, he gave
them a copy of the inspired writings, and continued on his
journey. In this way he gave birth to countless new communities. Quadratus was a man of exceptional ambition and ability
who could have risen to the heights of worldly wealth, power
and fame; but he directed all his ambition and ability to the
services of Christ.

Papias was a man of very limited intelligence, who frequently made mistakes in interpreting the sacred writings. For example, he got the idea that a thousand years after the birth of Christ, God will again send his Son down to earth, as ruler of all the nations; and there will then be a thousand years of peace. But, despite his mistakes, we owe a great debt to Papias. He grew to adulthood after all the first apostles had died. But he eagerly sought out the pupils of those apostles, and listened intently to everything they had to say. Indeed it was Papias' great and outstanding virtue that he preferred to listen than to speak. Thus it is from Papias that we learn of the source which Mark used in composing his gospel, namely the apostle Peter. Papias visited Mark, and learnt from him that Peter used to adapt his teaching to the occasion, quoting the words of Jesus Christ as they came into his mind. After some years Peter had no recollection of the circumstances in which Jesus spoke each particular parable or piece of wisdom, nor of the order in which each saying came. Thus Mark felt justified in composing a narrative which faithfully recorded all the sayings of Jesus but whose historical accuracy may be doubted.

As the gospel began to spread across the world, and as the churches shone like dazzling lights in dark places, so the devil, the sworn enemy of truth, turned all his weapons against the churches. Persecution was not his sharpest sword; indeed persecution, by demonstrating the serene courage of those who submit to martyrdom, often attracted more people to the gospel. The devil's most terrible weapon is distortion of the truth, which can pull even the most devout and faithful disciples from the straight path. Thus in the second century all manner of strange twisted ideas arose, which had the outward appearance of truth, but inwardly were full of lies. And the men who propounded these ideas, like Menander and Basilides, were handsome, intelligent and eloquent, so they easily lured people into their web of deceit. Once a person showed interest in their ideas, these men would then take them away from their families to special houses, where they would fill their minds with their lies. For five years these new followers were not allowed to speak or have any contact with the outside world. So by the time they emerged from these houses their minds and hearts were completely enslaved to falsehood; and they in turn could go out and lure others into the same web.

13

The pagan authorities were at times appallingly cruel to the Christians, and at times just. One provincial governor who showed justice was Serennius Granianus. He was deeply impressed by the courage which Christians showed in the face of death. He concluded that, contrary to wicked report, the Christians could not be seekers after pleasure. He thus wrote a letter to Emperor Hadrian posing these questions: 'How could a self-indulgent person, concerned only with physical pleasure, greet death with a smile, as if he wanted to be deprived of the things he loved most? Would he not strive by every means to prolong his present existence by denying his faith, rather than give himself up to certain death?' He then urged the Emperor to annul the law which made the profession of the Christian faith a capital offence. The Emperor did not accede to this request. But he did make it illegal for those in authority to offer financial rewards to people who betrayed Christians. As a result far fewer Christians were reported to the authorities, and so the number of martyrdoms fell for a time. This proved that those who betrayed Christians were generally motivated by the prospect of financial gain.

14

A man called Marcus invented a very strange baptism ceremony. It took place in a room that was fitted out like a bridal chamber, with a large bed draped in the most exquisite and expensive cloth. In the middle of the chamber was a bowl of water. The person to be baptized was taken to the bowl of water where he or she was stripped naked; the priest washed the naked body from head to foot. As he did so, the priest said: 'I baptize you in the name of the unknown Father of the universe, into Truth the Mother of all things, and into the divine Spirit who came down into Jesus.' The priest then led the person to the bed, where the person lay down. This was to show that baptism leads to a spiritual union, akin to the physical union of marriage, between Christ and the person who has received baptism. One can easily imagine the profound impact which such a ceremony had on those who participated in it.

15

The Christians in Asia Minor often encountered bitter hostility from the local population, so they wrote to Emperor Marcus Aurelius for protection. In response the Emperor wrote to the authorities in the province: 'Put your trust in the gods, not in your own strength; it is their task, nor yours, to detect and punish those who defy their wise laws. Stop accusing the Christians of atheism; such an accusation merely strengthens their faith. Your accusation is visibly false, since no atheist would go to his death with the same serene joy as a Christian does; this joy comes from a belief that their God will restore them to life. Thus when you send them to their deaths, they are the true winners: they believe they will live beyond death, and their joy attracts more people to their faith. I am aware that many earthquakes have been occurring in your province. It has not escaped my attention that when these earthquakes occur, your courage fails and your rule becomes weak, because you fear that our gods are punishing you. What a shameful contrast your cowardice makes with the courage which Christians show in the face of death. So instead of persecuting the Christians, learn from their example: let your faith in our gods be as strong as their faith in their God.'

16

Polycarp was appointed by the apostles themselves to be bishop of Smyrna. He lived a long time, and as a very old man he laid down his life by a most glorious and splendid martyrdom. Polycarp was warned in advance that the soldiers knew where he was staying, and were coming to arrest him. His friends begged him to escape. At first he refused to move, saying that he welcomed a martyr's death; but finally he agreed to go with them to a farm a short distance from the city. There he remained with a few companions, praying day and night for the churches throughout the world, imploring God to grant them peace. Three nights before his arrest, while he was at prayer, he saw in a dream the pillow under his head burst into flames and burn to a cinder. He awoke at once and interpreted the dream as meaning that he would depart this life by fire. The following day news came that the soldiers searching for Polycarp were near the farm, so his friends compelled him to move to another farm. He slept only two nights there. Late the next day, while Polycarp was upstairs praying, the soldiers arrived. They seized two servants and began to torture them by poking their swords through the skin of their naked stomachs. Polycarp heard what was happening; and to stop the torture he came downstairs and gave himself up to the soldiers.

As Polycarp walked slowly down the stairs of the farmhouse, he smiled at the soldiers who had come to arrest him. They were astonished to find that he was so old and frail. 'Why are the authorities so anxious to arrest such a man – what harm could he do?' they asked one another. Polycarp ordered that the table of the farmhouse be laid, and invited the soldiers to eat as much as they liked. While they served themselves, Polycarp stood in a corner of the room, and sang praises to God. The soldiers became so distressed at the prospect of such a saintly old man being sent to a cruel death, that they stopped eating. After an hour Polycarp stopped praying, and asked the soldiers to arrest him and take him to the city. They led him to Herod, who demanded that he make a sacrifice to the Emperor. Polycarp said nothing, and refused to move. 'What harm is there in offering a sacrifice to Caesar?' Herod demanded, his voice trembling with rage. Again Polycarp remained silent and motionless. Then Herod shouted at the old man: 'Unless you make a sacrifice to Caesar here and now, the soldiers will take you to the stadium, and there you will die.' Polycarp turned to the soldiers and beckoned to them to take him to the stadium.

As Polycarp was led into the stadium, he heard a voice from heaven, saying to him: 'Be strong, Polycarp, be strong.' As the crowd saw the frail old man, they let out a great roar; they were shocked to watch this gentle, loving Bishop being subjected to such a fate. The proconsul in the stadium urged Polycarp to renounce his faith: 'You need only say, "I deny Christ", and you will be safe.' 'I have been Christ's servant for eighty-six years,' replied Polycarp; 'he has always loved me and blessed me. How can I curse him now?' 'Turn to the people, then,' said the proconsul, 'and defend your faith before them.' 'The people already know me, and they know whose servant I am. Each one in the crowd may become a fellow-servant at any time he or she chooses.' At this the proconsul became angry. 'I have wild beasts,' he shouted; 'I will throw you to them if you persist in your attitude.' 'Call the wild beasts,' replied Polycarp; 'I cannot change my attitude if it means a change from better to worse. Yet you can change your attitude from cruelty to justice.' 'If you make light of the beasts,' roared the proconsul, 'I will have you destroyed by fire.' Polycarp replied: 'The fire you threaten burns for a time and is then extinguished. The fire which frightens me – and should frighten you – burns for ever.'

The proconsul now ordered logs and faggots to be collected from the public baths, where they were used to heat the water. When the pyre was ready Polycarp took off all his outer garments. Then he bent down to remove his shoes; but at that moment two of his companions rushed out from the crowd to help him. In the middle of the pyre was a stake, and the proconsul ordered the soldiers to nail him to it. 'There is no need for nails,' Polycarp cried out; 'he who will welcome me into his heavenly kingdom will also enable me to endure the fire without shrinking.' Polycarp stood with his back to the stake, and put his hands behind him to hold on to the stake. He looked like a noble ram taken from a great flock, being offered as a sacrifice to God. Then Polycarp prayed out loud: 'O Father of your beloved and blessed Son, Jesus Christ, through whom we have come to know you; O God of all creation, and of the whole family of the righteous who live in your presence: I bless you for counting me worthy of this day and this hour, that I may partake of Christ's cup, and then join the noble army of martyrs. I praise you and glorify you, now and forever.' The soldiers now lit the fire and a great flame shot up. The fire took the shape of a vaulted room; and Polycarp's body seemed not like burning flesh, but like gold and silver being refined in a furnace.

The ordinary people – the peasants and the artisans – were never enemies of the gospel. Many were indifferent: they were too concerned with earning their bread to consider religious questions; and, besides, they did not like to argue or make false statements about subjects they did not understand. A few, however, took time off from their work to learn about Jesus Christ, and were then converted; and these simple, un-educated people formed the majority in most churches. The greatest enemies were those educated in philosophy and rhetoric. They enjoyed trying to find flaws in the gospel, even though they rarely made the effort to study it properly. They despised Jesus Christ himself as a mere carpenter, and they thus treated Christianity with contempt, as a religion fit only for peasants and artisans. Indeed, they pointed to the large number of such people in the churches as a proof of this contention. Yet the real reason for their hostility to the gospel was that they hated the strict moral teaching which Christ gave and to which Christians adhered. Most philosophers loved to indulge their depraved sexual appetites, especially their lust for boys; so they hated a religion which condemned such behaviour.

In the year 165 Melito became bishop of Sardis. He was the first person to draw up a list of ancient Hebrew books which Christians should regard as their Old Testament. He also wrote a letter to Emperor, Marcus Aurelius, pleading for justice in the treatment of Christians: 'Our way of thought first sprung up amongst the Hebrew people, but it flowered amongst your own people in the glorious reign of your ancestor Augustus. It became to your empire a portent for good, because from that moment onwards Rome grew in splendour and power. To that power you have most happily succeeded; and it will remain with you and your son, if you protect this way of thought. The Christian faith has grown in stature as Rome has grown in power; and the two will continue to grow, so long as Rome respects Christianity. Christians for their part have from the beginning been exemplary in upholding the laws of your empire, and can justly claim to be your most loyal citizens. We do not ask any special favours. On the contrary, we ask only to be treated with the same respect which you and your ancestors have conferred on all the cults which flourish in your empire. We know that you are a man of deep philosophic insight and wide human sympathy; we trust that you will accede to our request.'

A wife and a husband both led dissolute lives, gratifying their sexual appetites with servants and slaves. The woman then came to know the gospel, and she reformed her ways. She tried to convince her husband of the truth of the gospel, but he was so deep in the pit of depravity that she was unable to lift him out. She now felt it wrong to continue sharing her bed with a man who so wilfully defied God's law, and she decided to end the marriage. But her family implored her to remain with him, in the hope that one day he would change; and she forced herself to stay. Sadly her husband became ever more depraved, and at last she could bear it no longer. One night she slipped out of the house, and the next day sent a messenger to her husband, informing him that she wished to divorce him. Her husband was furious, and accused her publicly of being a Christian. The local governor was a man who abided by the law in every particular. He informed the husband that he had a claim. Either the man could press charges; in which case he would have to acknowledge that he and the woman were divorced, and so he would be compelled to return the dowry. Or he could withdraw the charges, and contest the divorce; in which case he could keep the dowry. The man dropped the charges; so he kept the dowry and the woman kept her life.

23

Ptolemy was a man of the highest intellectual calibre, who was well versed in philosophy. And after much study he concluded that the teaching of Christ offered answers to the questions which the great philosophers of old had pondered. Word soon spread round the city that Ptolemy, who was much respected for his ability, had become Christian. And when this news reached the city prefect, he sent soldiers to arrest Ptolemy. The soldiers brought Ptolemy before the prefect who asked him a single question: 'Are you a Christian?' Ptolemy replied simply, 'Yes'. The prefect ordered the soldiers to tie a chain tightly around Ptolemy's body, and asked him again: 'Are you a Christian?' And Ptolemy said, 'Yes'. The prefect ordered the chain to be pulled tighter, so some of Ptolemy's ribs snapped. He asked the same question and received the same answer. The chain was pulled even tighter, so the rest of Ptolemy's ribs cracked, and he could hardly breathe. The same question was asked and the same answer given. At this point a man called Lucius, one of the prefect's assistants, stepped forward and said: 'I cannot watch Ptolemy's sufferings and remain silent. I too am a Christian.' So a chain was tied round Lucius also. And both men were crushed to death for their faith.

Those congregations which had never been seduced by false teachers were known as virgins. There were two simple signs which showed whether a false teacher had taken control of a church. The first could be observed at worship. A true teacher always wanted people to hear week by week extracts from the letters of Peter, Paul, Clement, Ignatius and the old great masters of the gospel. A false teacher by contrast banished such letters from worship, to keep the congregation in ignorance of their contents; in this way he could assert his own pernicious doctrines. The second could be observed when a traveller arrived. A congregation under a true teacher always had ample funds set aside to provide food for travellers, and for all those in need. A false teacher by contrast ensured that all surplus funds went into his own purse; so the congregation under his direction never had sufficient funds for travellers and for those in need. We should ask whether our own congregations today show signs of truth or falsehood. Are the letters of Peter, Paul and the rest read out week by week at worship? Are there ample funds for travellers and for the needy?

In Gaul two rumours spread about the Christians there. The first was that they were cannibals who, at their meetings for worship, gorged human flesh. This was a misunderstanding of the eucharist in which, in bread and wine, we share the body and blood of our Saviour. The second was that they were guilty of incest. This was because we call each other brother and sister; thus the married couples in the congregations were assumed to be siblings. These slanders gained greater currency because the authorities in Gaul arrested the domestic servants in Christian households, and then forced them under torture to affirm that they had witnessed cannibalism and incest. On one occasion an especially devout Christian called Vettius was accused of both these crimes, on the testimony of one of his servants. Since his conversion Vettius had been scrupulous in observing all the laws and commandments of Christ, and had been untiring in his service towards his neighbours, Christians and pagans alike. He publicly pleaded with the servant who had testified against him to speak the truth. The servant, whom Vettius had always treated with the utmost generosity, broke down in tears, and withdrew his testimony. At this the servant was also condemned as a Christian, and was executed with Vettius. A few minutes before his death, the servant asked Vettius for baptism; and with his final cup of water Vettius performed the ceremony.

Blandina was a young woman from a pagan family who became a Christian. She did not possess good looks; on the contrary, her face was ugly, and her body big and ungainly. Her father spent many years trying to find a man willing to marry her, offering the most generous dowry as an incentive; but to no avail. When Blandina became a Christian she told her father no longer to seek a husband for her, as she wished to remain a virgin for Christ's sake. Although her father was relieved that he would not have to pay a dowry, he was furious about her new faith. 'Why could you not be a virgin at the temple of Vesta?' he demanded. 'Because I have committed myself to Christ,' she replied. In his rage he reported her to the authorities, and they arrested her. Although she was ugly in body, she proved to possess a most beautiful spirit. She was tried and sentenced to death along with twenty other Christians. As Blandina and these other Christians stood outside the arena, waiting to be thrown to the wild beasts, Blandina led them in singing joyful hymns to Jesus. Thus when they were pushed into the arena and attacked by the beasts, they were all smiling serenely. And Blandina was still singing when all her four limbs had been torn from her body.

The story of the pastor Sanctus is a testimony to God's power of turning adversity to advantage. When he was arrested he refused to give his name, birthplace and nationality. Instead to every question he replied: 'I am a Christian.' The governor became so furious at this stubbornness, that he ordered his torturers to press red-hot copper plates against the most sensitive parts of his body. In the pain his whole body went into a spasm, becoming twisted and bent; but his soul remained straight and unyielding. At the end of the torture his body remained twisted so that he could not stand up or even lie down; he was like a spear that had been hammered by a blacksmith into a strange shape. Yet still the governor was not satisfied: 'I will not rest until this man gives me his name and birthplace – and renounces his faith.' So the torturers put Sanctus on a rack, and slowly turned the handle, pulling has head and his legs apart. As they did this, he body straightened out, healing his injuries. So when they took him off the rack, he could stand up and walk. The governor became so afraid of the Christian God that he immediately released Sanctus, who continued to be a faithful Christian pastor until he died many years later of natural causes.

Occasionally when a Christian was brought into a public place for trial or execution, the crowd were sympathetic and begged for his or her life to be spared. This happened when the Christian was well known for works of charity throughout the neighbourhood. But usually the crowd was hostile, calling for the most cruel forms of torture and death. Yet strangely the crowd was most hostile towards those who, under torture or the threat of death, denied their faith. The crowd then accused them of cowardice; and sometimes, after such people were released, the crowd would beat them to death. Those who were released and escaped subsequent death then descended into a pit of misery. They felt so ashamed of themselves that they dared not show themselves in public, nor return to their congregations. They became lonely and dejected, and usually died soon afterwards, their hearts broken by their denial of Christ. So even in this world there was more happiness, and less pain, in remaining loyal to the faith than in deserting it. And in the world to come the joy of the martyrs is pure and boundless.

Sometimes the authorities tortured Christians, inflicting the severest wounds, and then released them, in the hope that the sight of such terrible mutilations would demoralize other Christians. So these tortured Christians would return to their churches, their skin burnt, and their bones broken. Their brothers and sisters in Christ nursed them with such love and care that frequently they were restored to health – although usually, like the scars from the nails in our risen Lord's flesh, scars from their tortures remained visible. These men and women were hailed by their brothers and sisters as martyrs, since they had endured all the pain of martyrdom without its fulfilment. They themselves, however, wanted no special title, but to be treated as no different from any other Christian. 'It is God's grace, not our strength, which enabled us to endure the tortures inflicted on us,' they would say. This humility enabled them to show special mercy towards those who under torture had denied their faith. They would go to these people and pray with them, begging God to show them a sign of forgiving love. Then they would encourage them to return to their churches, and to continue worshipping Christ.

Alcibiades was a man who practised the most extreme austerity. He allowed himself only two or three hours sleep each night, spending the other hours of darkness in prayer. He wore only a few rags, sufficient to cover his nakedness but providing no warmth against the harsh winter winds. And he ate only bread and drank only water. He was arrested as a Christian. But his austerities had made his body virtually incapable of feeling pain, so he endured the tortures without flinching. The prefect who was trying him became so frustrated at his tranquillity that he decided to throw him into prison, in the hope that living in a dark dungeon amidst rats would weaken his spirit. But Alcibiades showed the same indifference towards prison as he had towards torture. Finally in despair the prefect released him. Then on his release a strange thing happened. Alcibiades decided that, by practising such extreme austerity, he was denying himself the wonderful material gifts that God had bestowed on humanity, and so he was showing ingratitude to God. Moreover this austerity had denied him the crown of martyrdom. So Alcibiades began to eat and sleep normally, and wear proper clothes. Some time later he was arrested again, and suffered acute pain when he was tortured. He then received the martyr's crown.

Under Emperor Antoninus persecutions continued, but without the same ferocity as before. This Emperor also wanted to put the mutual loyalty of Christians to good use in the service of the empire. So he formed a special legion of soldiers, which only Christians could join. Many young Christians were willing to offer themselves as soldiers, in order to show that their religious faith was compatible with good citizenship. Wisely Antoninus did not require his Christian soldiers to make any profession of devotion to him personally; he demanded only that they were obedient to their military commanders. This Christian legion soon won plaudits for its bravery and skill in battle. On one occasion they and some other legions were attacked by barbarians at dusk, after marching all day. It was high summer, and the soldiers had already drunk all their water; so their throats were so dry that they hardly had enough strength to lift their swords. The Christians fell on their knees in prayer. The enemy were astonished to see this; and they were even more astonished when at that moment the sky roared with thunder, and a torrent of rain began to fall. The barbarians fled in terror, and the soldiers quenched their thirst. From then onwards the Christian legion was known as the Thundering Legion.

During the second century the most common heresy, known as the 'Knowledge', was that Jesus Christ only had the appearance of flesh and blood, but in fact was pure spirit. The foundation of this heresy was a certain form of philosophy, which taught that God, who is infinite and eternal, could not possibly be joined with that which is finite and temporal. Those who held this heresy believed that salvation consisted in making the soul detached from all sensation of pleasure and pain; in this way the soul would gradually break free of the flesh, and be joined with God. This heresy had all sorts of evil consequences. Its proponents were indifferent to the material needs of others, saying that these needs were illusory; and so they showed no generosity. Worse still, they created a hier-archy, depending on the degree of detachment from bodily sensation which an individual had achieved. Since this detachment was supposed to lead to spiritual 'knowledge', those who became detached were exalted as teachers and prophets. These false teachers could then exert great power over the others, and often treated them like slaves. Needless to say, those who claimed to have acquired 'knowledge' often proved to be still strongly attached to bodily sensations; and they frequently used their followers for their own gratification.

A school was formed in Alexandria for pagans who were interested to learn more about Christianity. Since Alexandria contained many people well versed in pagan philosophy, the teachers at the school were themselves trained in philosophy, and sought to show that the gospel of Christ was fully compatible with the great philosophies of old. The school was headed at this time by Pantaenus, a scholar whose intellectual ability was respected by everyone in the city. As a young man he had been trained in the philosophy known as Stoicism. This philosophy teaches that in every object God's Logos is present; Logos gives each object its essential quality. At the same time each object has its own particular Pneuma, which gives it energy and action. The same Logos present in every object is also present within every person; and our primary purpose on earth is to achieve harmony between ourselves and all external objects, by recognizing and affirming the Logos which all people and objects share. In practice this means aligning our own Pneuma with the Pneuma of all people and objects around us. Achieving this harmony is what the Stoics called wisdom. Pantaenus taught that the way of Christ leads to perfect wisdom.

Pantaenus, the head of the Christian school of philosophy in Alexandria, taught that in Christ the universal, divine Logos, present in all people and objects, became fully manifest. This is because in the flesh and blood of Christ the Pneuma – the energy and action – was in complete unity and harmony with the divine Logos. Thus in Christ we see perfect wisdom. The perfect wisdom of Christ meant that he could never injure or harm others, because that would cause disharmony; instead he was impelled always to love and uphold them, and so enable them to grow in this same wisdom. Equally the perfect wisdom of Christ meant that he could never truly be injured by others: no amount of physical damage or psychological torment could destroy his inner peace. When Christ spoke of his perfect unity with the Father, he meant that he fully recognized and affirmed that the Logos within his own self was the divine Logos present throughout the universe. Thus he can guide us towards this same perfect unity, by enabling us to look inwards, and recognize our own essential unity with every person and every object. According to Pantaenus, to be perfectly wise is to be perfectly loving.

35

Jesus Christ was a humble carpenter, and his first disciples were peasants and fishermen. His teaching was wonderfully simple, so that people with no education could understand him as fully as those whose minds had been moulded by the arts of philosophy and logic. Indeed, as Christ himself acknowledged, uneducated people were often better able to understand the gospel, because the educated people could not accept that God's truth could be as simple as Christ said. For this reason, as the gospel spread across the world, educated Greeks and Romans initially treated it with contempt. They dismissed it as a fool's faith, fit only for the peasants and artisans from whom it had sprung. The Christian school of philosophy in Alexandria demonstrated for all to see that this contempt was itself great folly. Pantaenus, its head, and most of the teachers, had themselves grown up as pagans, and been educated in pagan philosophy. They came to see for themselves that the questions which Socrates, Plato and Aristotle had left unanswered were answered by Christ. And, by passing this insight to others, they compelled people to respect Christianity. Even the most hard-hearted pagan intellectual, who refused to accept Christianity for himself, was forced to accept that the arguments in its favour were strong.

In the church at Ardabau in Phrygia a new convert called Montanus suddenly fell into a trance during an act of worship. At first in tones of extreme excitement he talked nonsense which no one could understand; then he began to utter all sorts of strange prophecies. Some of those who heard Montanus were annoyed at his behaviour because it disrupted the tranquillity of their worship, and because they believed that he was possessed by an evil spirit. During the service itself they tried to restrain him, and afterwards they rebuked him severely. Others, however, were deeply impressed, believing that the Holy Spirit had conferred on Montanus a great gift. Montanus repeated his actions at the next service, talking nonsense and then uttering strange prophecies. This led to an irreconcilable division in the congregation. Those who believed that Montanus was possessed by an evil spirit asserted that he should no longer be allowed to attend worship, until the evil spirit had left him and he had repented. The others wanted Montanus to become leader of the church. Thus from that time onwards the two groups in Ardabau met separately. The group led by Montanus rapidly grew in number attracting new members week by week. The other group gradually dwindled.

The style of worship favoured by Montanus and his followers proved very popular; and it is easy to understand the reason. The services were spiritual orgies. Instead of long sermons, in which the meaning of scriptural passages was expounded in detail, people shouted out single sentences which they claimed were divine prophecies. Instead of reciting the psalms contained in scripture, they chanted phrases which they themselves composed; and they danced and waved their arms. Instead of offering prayers which had been written by the great fathers of the church, they just prayed in their own words. Even women were permitted to stand up and speak, saying whatever they wished. Not only did Montanus' own congregation in Ardabau expand rapidly, but congregations throughout Asia abandoned the conventional style of worship, and adopted Montanus' style. In itself there was nothing wrong with the spiritual freedom which these congregations enjoyed. We know that the Holy Spirit can bestow all manner of different spiritual gifts; and the members of these congregations were sincerely wishing to receive and use these gifts. But as their number expanded they became contemptuous of more conventional congregations, calling them 'prophet-killers'. Also their leaders no longer felt constrained by the scriptures or the teachings of the fathers in what they taught; so they frequently led their congregations astray.

The number of congregations who followed Montanus continued to grow throughout Asia, and spread to other parts of the world also. Many people within these congregations benefited greatly, learning to praise and pray to God with all their hearts and minds. But after some decades many began to go astray. Their leaders, who accepted no authority beyond themselves – because they believed themselves always to be guided directly by God – became corrupt. Some kept for themselves the gold and the silver which their congregations donated; so instead of using this money to help the poor, they lived in great luxury, building fine houses for themselves, eating fine food, and dressing in robes fit for princes. Others used their spiritual power to exploit women in their congregations, gratifying their illicit sexual appetites. At first their congregations made no objection, imagining that this evil behaviour must sanctioned by God. But eventually some began to question their leaders; and, when the leaders refused to answer the questions, many left. Also the flow of new members dried up. So the churches died. The lesson from this is that all people, even the most able leaders, must test the guidance which they believe God is giving by consulting the church and submitting to its authority.

At the end of the second century a great controversy arose about the date of Easter. In Asia they followed the ancient tradition of beginning the Paschal festival on the fourteenth day of the lunar month, the day on which the Jews had been commanded to sacrifice the lamb. They observed this date regardless of the day of the week on which it fell. But nowhere else in the world kept to this tradition. In accordance with the teachings of the apostles, they believed that Easter should always be celebrated on the first day of the week, when the Saviour was raised. Thus year by year they adjusted the date of Easter accordingly. To try and resolve this controversy a special synod was held, in which the apostolic tradition was upheld without dissent. But none of the Asian bishops were present, so many Asian churches did not accept this decision. Victor, the head of the Roman church, wrote to all the Asian churches, ordering them to observe the apostolic tradition regarding the date of Easter. And in his letter he referred to many former bishops of Asian churches who themselves had followed the apostolic tradition.

When the Asian churches received the letter from the Bishop of Rome, ordering them to change the way in which they set the date for Easter, they were incensed. They did not recognize the authority of the Roman bishop to issue such an order. But their objection had a deeper purpose. In their view the date of Easter was utterly irrelevant; they believed that churches should be permitted to celebrate Easter whenever they wished. They took the same attitude in relation to the fast prior to Easter. As they observed in their reply to the Bishop of Rome: 'Some think they should fast for one day, some for two, others for still more; some make their fast last for forty hours, to reflect the forty days Jesus spent in the wilderness. Such variation did not originate in our own day, but much earlier, in the time of our forefathers who had no regard for strict accuracy. In spite of these differences of practice, they all lived in peace with one another. So should we today: diversity in these outward practices strengthens the unity of our inner faith.' This attitude was unacceptable to the Bishop of Rome, who believed that unity of faith required uniformity of practice. Thus the difference over the dating of Easter between the eastern and the western churches persisted.

41

A shoemaker in Rome called Theodotus started to teach that
Jesus Christ was not divine, but merely human. Although his
profession was humble, Theodotus had learnt to read, and had
been skilled in philosophy and logic. He pointed to various
texts in scripture which showed that through his childhood
Jesus grew in wisdom and insight. Theodotus argued that, if
Jesus had been divine, he would have possessed perfect
wisdom from the moment of his birth. Thus the fact that he
grew in wisdom suggests that he was in his childhood
imperfect – and that he achieved perfection through prayer
and through acts of love. Theodotus further argued that his
views strengthened, rather than weakened, the power of the
gospel: if Jesus actually achieved perfection through the course
of his life, instead of being perfect from birth, it gives others
hope that they too can achieve perfection. Theodotus himself
was a man of exemplary character, devout in prayer and
constantly active in serving others. But the Bishop of Rome
perceived the dangers of Theodotus' teaching: that if Jesus was
merely human, he could not be worshipped; and the claim
that Christianity makes of being superior to all other faiths
would be void. Thus the Bishop, with great reluctance,
decided to excommunicate Theodotus.

Prior to his excommunication Theodotus the shoemaker had gained many followers. Indeed in almost every congregation in Rome and the surrounding area there were groups who shared Theodotus' view that Jesus Christ was not divine, but simply a human being who had achieved spiritual perfection. These groups became a source of deep division within these congregations, leading to many destructive and violent arguments. After Theodotus was excommunicated his followers formed a new sect, worshipping separately from whose who maintained the orthodox faith. And they appointed a man called Natalius as their bishop, paying him 150 denarii each month. However soon after his appointment the Lord started coming to Natalius in visions at night. The Lord warned Natalius that, by cutting himself off from the orthodox church, he risked condemning himself to eternal torment. At first Natalius was so proud of his position as bishop and so pleased with the income he was receiving, that he paid no attention to these visions. But one night holy angels came and whipped him; from midnight until dawn they lacerated his flesh with ropes. When he arose there were no visible wounds, but he was in terrible agony. So he sprinkled his body with ashes and put on sackcloth, and went to the true Bishop of Rome. He fell on his knees before the Bishop, and begged to be received back into the orthodox church. The Bishop questioned Natalius closely to ensure that his repentance was sincere; then he welcomed him back. Soon afterwards most other members of the sect were begging to be readmitted to the orthodox church. The sect collapsed, and Theodotus died in misery.

A group of Christians arose who tried to re-write the teaching of Christ and of Paul as a series of syllogisms. Their god was not the God to whom Christ referred, but logic; they made an idol out of reasoned argument. This meant that they ignored all those parts of scripture which could not be fitted into their logical scheme, and used only those parts which could be reduced to syllogisms. Another group arose which tried to express the teachings of Christ and Paul in the form of diagrams. Their god was geometry, and their saviour Euclid. They too ignored parts of the gospel which would not fit their geometrical scheme. Neither of these groups felt any guilt about selecting those parts of the gospel which they wanted, and setting aside the rest. They convinced themselves that the parts they chose were what truly mattered, and that the rest was quite unimportant. The error of both these groups was not lack of faith nor lack of sincerity, but a failure to appreciate the mystery of God. Although God is fully present in Jesus Christ, we are not able to see in him the fullness of God owing to our sinful natures. Thus we cannot reduce the divine truth to a series of logical statements or geometrical diagrams which our minds can grasp. Nor can we discriminate between different parts of scripture. Logic and geometry, and all our rational faculties, are only very partial and inadequate tools for discerning truth; they must be supplemented by the Holy Spirit, who can never be encapsulated within an intellectual system.

When Severus became emperor late in the second century a new persecution began, more cruel and relentless than anything which had gone before. In the tenth year of the reign of Severus a boy was born in Alexandria who was destined to become one of the greatest visionaries in the history of Christianity. By now the flames of persecution had been fanned into a great blaze: and even as a child Origen longed for martyrdom. When Origen was aged seventeen, his father Leonides, who was a devout Christian, was arrested and sentenced to death. As soon as Origen heard his father had been put in prison, he decided to go to the authorities and declare that he too was a Christian, and so should die with his father. His mother implored him not to go, saying that she could not bear to lose both her husband and her son. Yet even his mother's pleas did not quench his thirst for a martyr's death. So she hid all his clothing; and this forced him to stay at home. Instead he sent a letter to his father in prison, urging him to remain strong in the face of torture. He concluded the letter with these words: 'Mind you do not change your mind on our account.'

After Leonides had been martyred, his property was seized for the imperial treasury. So Origen, his mother and his six younger brothers found themselves destitute. Origen was a very handsome young man and witty in conversation. Happily a wealthy widow, herself a Christian, made herself Origen's patron, providing him and his family with a small house in which to live and food to eat. Origen was now able to devote himself fully to study. As he read the scriptures he came to believe that, beneath the obvious meaning of each word and sentence, there were deeper levels of meaning; and that the task of the Christian scholar was to penetrate those meanings. This must be done by a combination of intellectual reflection and profound prayer. In this way the individual could enter the mystery of God himself, and reach a direct vision of the divine glory. He also steeped himself in pagan philosophy, partly because he recognized that the ancient masters possessed much wisdom, and partly in order to be able to teach the gospel to the pagan intellectuals in Alexandria. Against the wishes of his wealthy patron, who wanted to cosset him, he imposed the strictest discipline on himself. In obedience to our Saviour's teaching, he had only one cloak and one pair of shoes. He slept on the floor without blankets, and often rose after a few hours to pray. He ate simply, fasted regularly and abstained from wine.

As the persecutions grew more severe, Origen made himself into a pastor to those destined for martyrdom. When they were in prison he found ways of visiting them, sometimes by dressing up as a palace guard. When they were being tried, he would offer himself as their advocate, using his sharp wit to trounce their accusers. And when they were led out to die, he was at their side, praying with them and comforting them. He himself had no fear of death; on the contrary he longed to be a martyr. But for the sake of other martyrs he made every effort to preserve his own life. So he moved from house to house, never staying in one place more than a few nights; and he wore all manner of disguises to conduct his work as pastor. To the fury of the authorities, his intellectual flair won the respect of many pagan scholars in the city; and they came to him in increasing numbers to learn about Christianity. They surmised that if a man of Origen's mental and spiritual calibre could espouse this new religion, it must contain some important truths. Thus Origen became principal of an academy for Christian philosophy; and he held classes in all sorts of secret places, to avoid detection. Many of his pupils became Christians; and of these many suffered martyrdom.

In addition to pagan philosophers, Origen accepted as pupils women of all ages who wanted to learn about the Christian faith. One of these was Potamiaena, a young woman of immense beauty. She had received numerous offers of marriage, but wished to dedicate her life to the pursuit of truth; and for this purpose she sought out Origen. Through him she became a Christian. But when her father discovered her conversion he was enraged, and reported her to the authorities. She was immediately arrested and put on trial. Aquila, the judge, subjected her to the most terrible tortures, and even handed her over to the gladiators to be raped. But she remained calm and tranquil, constantly reaffirming her faith in Christ. Finally Aquila sentenced her to die by have boiling pitch poured over her body. A soldier called Basilides was ordered to lead her to the place of execution. As the crowd pushed forward and shouted obscene insults at her, Basilides drove them away. He took her gently by the arm, and sought to comfort her. She thanked him for his kindness, and reassured him that Christ was giving her sufficient strength to endure her agonies. When they reached the place of execution she lay down on the ground. The torturer slowly poured the boiling pitch, drop by drop, over different parts of her body, until she was covered from head to toe. As her face disappeared beneath the pitch, she was joyfully singing God's praises.

Basilides, the soldier who led Potamiaena to her execution and comforted her, was deeply impressed by her joyful courage in the face of such terrible cruelty. Some time later Basilides and the other soldiers in his legion were required to renew their oath of allegiance to the Emperor, and affirm him as a god. Basilides declared that he was unable to do this, as he was now a Christian. At first his fellow soldiers thought he was joking; but when he stuck doggedly to his assertion, they took him to a magistrate. Basilides repeated his confession of faith, and the magistrate sent him to prison to await trial. When other Christians in the city heard about Basilides, they went to visit him, and asked him what had brought about his conversion. Basilides replied that three days after her martyrdom Potamiaena had appeared to him at night and put a wreath over his head; she then said that she had prayed for him to the Lord, and that soon the Lord would place him by her side. At this the Christian congregation baptized him; and the next day Basilides was beheaded. It is said that Potamiaena appeared to many other people in the city, and called them to embrace the gospel.

While giving Christian instruction in Alexandria, Origen did something which proved that his mind was youthful and immature, but that his faith was strong and his mastery over the body complete. He spent many day contemplating the words of Christ that 'there are those who make themselves eunuchs for the kingdom of God'. He was already anxious that his willingness to instruct young women, as well as men, might provoke vile rumours. He concluded that the only way of putting himself above suspicion was to take this saying literally; and with his own hand he emasculated himself. He tried to keep this act secret, but blood from the wound stained his cloak, causing his pupils to question him. Soon Demetrius, the bishop in Alexandria, heard what Origen had done. He chastised Origen for being headstrong, but commended his enthusiasm and his sincerity of faith. Some years later, when Origen had become famous throughout the world as a philosopher and theologian, Demetrius was consumed with envy and turned against him. Demetrius wrote to bishops in every place referring to Origen's youthful act, and claimed that it proved Origen to be insane.

50

During the reign of Severus as emperor, Narcissus was bishop in Jerusalem. He was renowned for the miracles he performed. For example, during the all-night vigil one Easter the deacons ran out of oil for their lamps. Narcissus ordered them to draw water from a nearby well, and pour it into their lamps; Narcissus then prayed over the lamps, and the water turned into oil. Narcissus also possessed in great measure the gift of discerning spiritual gifts. Thus he promoted to positions of leadership those best suited for this task, while passing over others who wanted power, but lacked the gift or the spiritual strength to exercise it. Some of those who wanted power became angry with Narcissus for refusing it, and they started spreading slander against him, accusing him of stealing church funds and of sexual immorality. When people questioned them about these accusations, one replied: 'If they aren't true, may I be burnt to death!' Another said: 'May my body be wasted by a foul disease!' A third said: 'May I lose my sight!' The faithful were not moved by these accusations, because they could see the unshakeable integrity and transparent goodness of Narcissus' character. But Narcissus himself was greatly distressed. So he left Jerusalem and fled into the desert.

Narcissus, having been driven from his church in Jerusalem by power-hungry rivals, went to live in a remote cave. Groups of his supporters went out into the desert to search for him, but none could find him. Everyone in Jerusalem, even his rivals, knew the power of Narcissus' prayers; and it now seemed that he was secretly praying for his rivals' destruction. One night a tiny spark settled on the roof of the leading rival, causing the thatch to catch fire; the whole house quickly burnt to ashes. Another rival caught a disease which caused his skin to peel off, leaving his flesh red and raw. A third became so frightened by what was happening that he came to the congregation and begged them to pray for him, in opposition to the prayers of Narcissus. As he pleaded tears flowed from his eyes with such force that he went blind. After Narcissus' departure the congregation had felt reluctantly compelled to appoint another bishop, called Dius. One day, after ten years in the desert, Narcissus returned, appearing amidst the congregation during their main act of worship. Dius was the first to greet him, and begged him to become bishop again. But Narcissus refused, saying: 'The opposition to my leadership made me bitter and angry, proving that I am not fit to be a bishop. My task is to pray for you and your successors.'

In Alexandria Origen's approach to scripture, in which he sought several deeper levels of meaning to each sentence and phrase, became very popular. Origen himself always checked that the deeper meanings which he suggested were in harmony with the obvious meaning; in his mind this was the main test of truth, since God could never contradict himself. But in less devout hands this method of interpretation was fraught with dangers, since people could suggest meanings which suited themselves, rather than reflected divine truth. Soon there were groups of Christians who, by distorting Origen's method, justified all manner of evil activities. This enabled the pagans in the city to launch a very powerful attack on the church. One of these pagans was called Porphyry; his attack was extremely subtle. He made a clear distinction between the Jewish scriptures, which he said were depraved, and the Christian scriptures – the gospels – which he admitted were essentially good. The goats, he said, are evil, and use Origen's method to distort the gospels, in order to justify their evil. The sheep are good, and use Origen's method to explain away the Jewish scriptures. He concluded that, since goats and sheep are mixed together in every congregation, it is wiser to avoid Christianity altogether.

53

In the middle of the third century a dispute arose over the authorship of two books which many regarded as written by apostles: the second epistle of Peter, and the epistle to the Hebrews. In both cases the objection was that the style did not conform to that of other works by Peter and Paul respectively. Shortly afterwards a dispute arose over the epistles attributed to John. While it was generally accepted that the apostle called John wrote the gospel attributed to him, and the Book of Revelation, the epistles were regarded as too slight and superficial to have been composed by such a magisterial hand. Many harsh and violent words were exchanged over these matters. Eventually a conclusion was reached which satisfied everyone. It was agreed that it was impossible to know for certain who was the author of these disputed works. However in each case the teaching contained within them was in complete harmony with the teaching in the authors' works which was beyond dispute. And since it is the inner meaning of the works which matters, not the outward style, the works should be accepted as genuine.

When Anteros, the bishop of the Roman church, died after only a month in office, the people were so distressed that when they gathered to elect a successor they were unable to think of anyone. So they decided to hold another meeting in four weeks' time. A few days later a Christian called Fabian, who was pastor to a small congregation in the remote countryside, arrived in Rome. He had heard of the death of Anteros, and wanted to express his condolences. The Roman Christians were grateful for Fabian's sympathy, and invited him to attend their meeting to elect a successor. By the time the meeting was held various people had already been suggested, all of them were eminent members of the congregation. For some hours there was heated debate, but they could not agree; in fact, the longer the debate continued, the deeper were the divisions between the supporters of different names. Then unexpectedly a dove flew in through a window, fluttered around the room, and then settled on the head of Fabian. Everyone took this as a sign of the Holy Spirit descending on the man; and with one voice they acclaimed him as their new bishop. He served for ten years, proving to be a man of profound sanctity and compassionate leadership.

55

Dionysius was one of the leaders of the church in Alexandria when Emperor Decius announced a new persecution. Immediately the governor of Alexandria despatched a military officer to arrest Dionysius. The officer imagined that, as soon as the persecution had been announced, Dionysius would have escaped from his home. So the officer searched along the roads and rivers, in fields and ditches, where he guessed Dionysius might be walking or hiding. But for four days Dionysius remained at home. Then he felt prompted by God to leave, taking a group of young men with him. One night they stayed near a village called Taposiris; and one of the young men called Timothy went out to buy food. The military officer, accompanied by a dozen well-armed soldiers, was searching the village that night, and discovered Dionysius and his companions. The officer was delighted that after such a long hunt he had found his prey. The soldiers tied Dionysius and his companions in chains, and dragged them to the small barracks on the outskirts of the village. There the officer took great pleasure in beating Dionysius with a stick and a whip. He also ordered large quantities of wine, for him and his men to celebrate their success. Soon the officer and his men were roaring drunk.

In the meantime Timothy returned, laden with food, to the house where Dionysius and his companions were staying. A servant of the house told Timothy what had happened. Timothy collapsed on the floor, tears pouring from his eyes; he was so devoted to his master Dionysius that he felt utterly helpless without him. The servant comforted him, urging him to get up and go in search of Dionysius and the others, in the hope of enabling them to escape. So Timothy left the house and stood in the village street, wondering how to begin his search. At that moment a man passed by, on his way to a wedding feast – in Egypt wedding feasts start in the evening and continue until dawn. Timothy asked the man if he knew the whereabouts of Dionysius and his companions. 'God has led you to me,' the man replied, 'because I too am a Christian, and so are the other guests at the feast I am attending. We have all heard of Dionysius' wonderful devotion to Christ. May God preserve him.' The man took Timothy to the feast, and announced to the other guests what had happened. They all immediately rose up, and marched to the barracks where Dionysius and his companions were being held. As they burst through the gates they shouted and yelled so loudly that the soldiers thought a large army of bandits was attacking them – and instantly fled. So Dionysius and his companions were saved – and all of them survived the persecution which Emperor Decius had ordered.

When the governor of Alexandria heard of the escape of Dionysius and his companions, he was enraged. He arrested the military officer and his men, and with his own hand pushed them off a bridge near the city into a deep ravine. Then he ordered his officers to search every house in the city for Christians. Fearing that they themselves might be out-witted – and so be pushed into a ravine – they began with the old people who were too frail to run away. First they seized an old man called Metras, and ordered him to utter blasphemies against Christ. When he refused they drove sharp reeds into his face and eyes; then they dragged him out of the city, and stoned him to death. Next they arrested Quinta, who at the age of eighty had just become a Christian. They tied her feet together, and then pulled her along the street, so her back bumped up and down on the cobbles. Soon all her old bones were broken and she died. They took Apollonia, a wonderful old lady who had been offering hospitality to tramps and vagabonds for sixty years. They led her to the central square and built a pyre. One soldier lit it, while two others knocked all her teeth out with sticks. The soldiers stood wondering what other tortures they could inflict before burning her. But while they wondered, she leapt from their clasp into the fire; and within a few seconds her tiny, old body was ashes.

After the military officers had arrested and killed the old Christians of Alexandria, they turned to the younger ones. At this point the governor issued a decree declaring that henceforth no Christian could work in public service, and that the public services should be purged of all Christians. So the officers marched on the public buildings throughout the city. It was well known amongst the public servants themselves who were Christian and who were not; so there was little hope of escaping detection. Most of the Christian public servants remained calmly at their posts, waiting to be dragged out. Great fires were lit in the streets, and these brave Christians were hurled one by one into the flames. The soldiers were deeply impressed at the calm dignity and courage with which these men faced death; and some of the soldiers secretly became Christians that very day. Sadly, however, some Christian public servants were so terrified that they rushed out, and ran towards a pagan altar to offer sacrifices. The soldiers could not arrest these people who had denied their faith. But they shouted insults at them, accusing them of cowardice, and they spat in their faces. The governor, too, despised their cowardice; and he dismissed them from public office, so they were reduced to poverty.

59

A few days later a boy aged fifteen, called Dioscorus, was arrested. The judge tried to trick him into denying his faith with clever words, but Dioscorus remained adamant that Christ, and Christ alone, was his master. Then the judge ordered the soldiers to inflict various kinds of torture on the boy to force him to deny Christ; but nothing would weaken Dioscorus' resolve. The judge now ordered some older Christians to be brought before him; and when these older Christians upheld their faith, the judge ordered the soldiers to tear them to pieces limb by limb, in front of Dioscorus' eyes. Yet still the boy stubbornly clung to his faith. Finally the judge dismissed him, saying that in view of his youth he would give him time to come to his senses. Dioscorus now used his freedom to help other Christians escape from the city into the countryside. Night by night he led groups of Christians through the dark streets, to caves and huts outside, from where they could travel in safety to Christian congregations in remote towns and villages. Dioscorus survived this persecution, and later became bishop of Alexandria. He lived to a great age, and died of natural causes.

The astonishing dignity and courage shown by so many of the Christians in the face of torture and death affected a growing number of soldiers who witnessed it. Many began to feel ashamed at what they were doing: they felt like cowards as they inflicted pain and death on people who carried no weapons and made no effort to resist. They concluded that the spiritual armour which these Christians wore was far stronger than the metal swords which they, as soldiers, wielded. As a result some soldiers actually submitted to Christ, and sought baptism. On one occasion three Christian soldiers, called Ammon, Zeus and Ingenuus, found themselves standing guard in court while a man called Theophilus was being tried. The three soldiers could see that under torture Theophilus' faith was weakening. So they started to grind their teeth to gain Theophilus' attention; then they stretched out their arms in imitation of Christ on the cross, to encourage Theophilus. But not only did Theophilus turn to look at them; everyone in the court stared in their direction. The three soldiers rushed to the dock to stand by Theophilus, and declared that they too were Christians. The three soldiers and Theophilus were sentenced to death by beheading, and marched out of the court towards the place of execution, singing a hymn of triumph.

The church in Rome suffered persecution under Decius as severe as that in Alexandria. One of those who managed to escape the city and survive was a priest called Novatus. When the persecution was over he returned to the city. The Bishop of Rome had been martyred, so the Christian congregation gathered to appoint a successor. Novatus had publicly declared that he did not wish to be bishop, saying that he was unworthy of such high office. But secretly he had bribed a number of people to propose him. In the middle of the meeting to appoint a new bishop, at a signal from Novatus, these people spoke one after the other, each proposing Novatus as bishop. The others in attendance did not suspect bribery or collusion, but took this unanimous call to be a sign from the Holy Spirit. So Novatus was made bishop. Immediately Novatus declared that all those who under torture had denied their faith should be permanently excluded from the church. He also required that every member of the church should declare allegiance to a series of doctrinal formulae which he himself composed. By these means, Novatus declared, the church would become pure. And he and his supporters called themselves 'Puritan'.

When Novatus declared that all who had denied their faith
under torture were to be permanently excluded from the
church, most Christians in Rome were appalled. The small
band of Christians who had kept their faith under torture, and
had subsequently escaped and survived, were especially
horrified. They humbly acknowledged that under their own
strength they could never have endured the torture, and that
only through God's grace had they remained loyal to Christ.
Thus they had particular sympathy for those who had
weakened. They went to Novatus and asserted their
opposition to his policy, adding: 'You yourself never suffered
torture for your faith; so you have no right to pass judgement
on those who have suffered.' Novatus not only dismissed their
arguments, but demanded that they submit to the doctrinal
test which he had devised, to ensure their faith was pure.
When they refused, he excommunicated them. The church in
Rome was now divided into two groups: those who
supported Novatus' policy; and those who wanted to offer the
hand of forgiveness and friendship to the men and women
who had denied their faith under torture. At first there were
equal numbers in both groups. But Novatus became
increasingly authoritative within his group, demanding total
and unquestioning obedience to his every command. He also
required his members to pay him large sums, in order for him
to have a veritable army of priests and servants in his
employment. In the face of these pressures people gradually
deserted him.

63

During the persecution under Decius a man called Serapion denied his faith under torture, and so escaped death. After the persecution was over his congregation offered to forgive him and welcome him back. But he was too ashamed of his weakness to respond; so he worshipped alone at home. Many years later, when he was an old man, he fell sick and for three days could not speak. On the fourth day his speech returned. He said to his grandson: 'I am about to die. Go and ask the Christian priest to come and see me.' The grandson went to the priest's house, and begged him to come and see his grandfather. But the priest had never heard of Serapion, and so feared that the boy's request might be some kind of malicious trick. So he refused to go. But in case the request was genuine, the priest went to the casket where the consecrated bread was kept, and took out a portion. 'Put this in your grandfather's mouth,' the priest said. The boy returned and gave his grandfather the bread. 'Ah,' the grandfather said, 'just as years ago I was too frightened of torture to do my duty, the priest is too frightened of being tricked to do his. By his fear I am forgiven.' The old man then ate the bread. 'At last Christ has come to me,' he whispered, and then died.

A man from Libya called Sabellius, who was well trained in philosophy, objected to the notion of the 'Trinity'. He claimed that God could not possibly have three persons, since a single unified being could not be divided into three parts. Instead he taught that there is one God, but we as humans perceive him in three ways; and we give him three names corresponding to these three aspects. Firstly we perceive God in his creation; and this aspect we call Father. Secondly we perceive him in the person of Jesus Christ; and this aspect we call Son. And thirdly we perceive him at work in the human soul; and this aspect we call Spirit. Sabellius gained many followers throughout the Christian world. At first few people objected to his teaching. But gradually a number of bishops and priests began to attack him as a heretic. In particular they said that if Jesus Christ is only a means of perceiving God, rather than God himself, there may be numerous other men and women who could also claim to be windows on God. Thus, they argued, Sabellius' teaching undermined the church's claim to be the sole and exclusive purveyor of divine truth. A synod of bishops was called, and the teaching of Sabellius was condemned.

Whenever a split occurs within the church, questions arise about the validity of baptism performed by those regarded as heretics. Xystus, as bishop in Rome, related an example of this. One day an old man came to him, his face streaked with tears. This man had been receiving communion week by week for many decades. Since his own baptism as a young man, he had not attended a service of baptism – until a few days before visiting Xystus. Then he went to the baptism of a young woman, and was deeply moved by the event. It brought back memories of his own baptism. At first these memories made him happy. But then he recalled that the priest who had baptized him had soon afterwards joined a heretical sect. The old man thus became convinced that his baptism could not have been valid; a priest who did not hold the true faith, the old man said to himself, could not possibly baptize someone into that faith. When the old man explained his anxieties, Xystus was at first perplexed, since he could see the force of the old man's arguments. He was on the point of offering to baptize the old man again, when it occurred to him that this could have disastrous consequences. If the validity of baptism depended on the quality of the priest's faith, Xystus said to himself, then countless thousands of Christians would share the old man's anxieties. Worse still, every baptism could be preceded by the candidate closely questioning the priest on doctrinal matters. So Xystus ruled that all baptisms are valid, regardless of the quality of the priest's faith.

In the middle of the third century the new Emperor Valerian seemed at first very tolerant towards Christians, and even encouraged the growth of churches. He openly acknowledged that Christians were almost invariably good citizens, working hard and abiding by the law. He even said that, if all his subjects were true Christians, the empire would flourish and prosper as never before. But then his attitude suddenly changed. He came under the influence of a group of magicians from Egypt. They persuaded him to adopt all sorts of evil practices, including the most immoral acts with young boys. They told the Emperor that these practices would give him supernatural strength. The magicians realized that the Emperor would resist the idea of a full-scale persecution of Christians. Instead they warned him that the presence of Christians in the major cities of the empire would weaken his power; and they urged him to exile all Christians to the desert. So Valerian issued a decree to this effect. The result was that tens of thousands of bishops, priests and lay people were pushed out into remote towns and villages. At first many Christians were very angry at this treatment. But many barbarians and uncivilized people who inhabited these remote regions were so impressed by the love and gentleness of these exiled Christians that they too adopted the faith. So the effect of Valerian's decree was to spread the faith to the farthest corners of the world.

A precise record has been preserved of the dialogue between Dionysius, the Bishop of Alexandria, and Aemilian, the governor of that city, in response to the decree from Emperor Valerian. 'The Emperor has always been kind and generous to Christians,' Aemilian began, 'and he now wants to continue this kindness. He does not want you to abandon the Christian God. He simply wants you to add to your services special prayers to the god who preserves his throne. To refuse this request would be ungrateful and mean.' 'Not all men worship all gods,' Dionysius replied; 'each worships some – those he believes in. We indeed worship the God who preserves the Emperor's throne, praying to him every day. He is the same God who created all things, and came to earth in Jesus Christ. Our Emperor may entrust himself, his throne, and his empire entirely to this God.' 'If this is the case,' Aemilian asked, 'why can you not use the same name for your god as the Emperor uses for his?' 'It is not the name which matters,' answered Dionysius, 'but the meaning. If you could assure us that the god whom Valerian worships is the same God who came to earth in Jesus Christ, we shall worship his god as our God.' Aemilian refused to give this assurance, and so sentenced Dionysius to exile.

Although Emperor Valerian did not want Christians to be tortured and executed for their faith, a soldier called Marinus in Caesarea received the martyr's crown. Marinus was a man of noble birth who had served the army with distinction. A centurion in his legion was forced to retire through sickness, and by order of seniority Marinus should have filled his place. But just as Marinus was about to be given the badge of office, the next in seniority stepped forward and denounced Marinus as a Christian. Marinus immediately confessed his faith. The governor of Caesarea, who was presiding at the ceremony, gave Marinus three hours to reflect on his position. The Bishop of Caesarea, who was present in the crowd, came to the front and took Marinus by the arm, leading him back to his house. A table stood in the centre of the house, and the Bishop asked Marinus to lay his sword on it. Then the Bishop placed a Bible beside the sword. 'With your right hand', the Bishop said, 'take which of the two – the sword or the Bible – you prefer.' Marinus immediately took the Bible. 'Hold fast to it then,' the Bishop said. Marinus now walked back to the governor clutching the Bible. The governor ordered Marinus to be beheaded; and even when Marinus' head rolled to the ground, his right hand still clung to the Bible.

Although Jews do not build statues of their heroes, the Greeks have always done so. Thus it is not surprising that in the city of Caesarea, which is mainly inhabited by Greeks, the Christians should have created a bronze statue of Jesus Christ. It is equally natural that they should have commemorated the incident when he cured the woman with a haemorrhage, because this woman came from Caesarea. Indeed the statue was erected outside this woman's house; and both the house and the statue still stand to this day. Around the base of the statue the Christians planted many exotic herbs, which continue to grow in great profusion. People of the city have from the start been invited to take leaves from these herbs, and to consume them as medicine to cure their illnesses. Many wonderful healings have occurred in this way. The herbs also give a most sweet aroma; and people have been healed of all manner of diseases simply by walking near the herbs, and smelling this aroma. It is impossible to say whether the statue of Christ has such a beneficial effect, or whether the properties of the herbs themselves are curative. But in either case the power of God is the true cause.

Eventually Emperor Valerian lost faith in the Egyptian magicians who had turned him against the Christians; and he issued a decree allowing Christians to return from exile to the cities. Soon afterwards a terrible plague broke out in many cities in the empire. At first people blamed the Christians, saying that their return had angered the gods. But their attitude changed when they saw how the Christians responded. The Christians had no fear of catching the dreaded disease themselves; and those who caught it embraced death with joyful anticipation. Free from fear, the Christians went out in pairs to visit every house which the plague had touched, and they offered to nurse those who had succumbed. This enabled the other members of the household to flee into the safety of the countryside. In this way many people embraced the faith. The sick became Christians in the final hours of their lives; with their dying breath they affirmed their faith, and then received baptism. Those who escaped were so grateful for their deliverance that after the plague was over, they sought out a priest and asked to be instructed in the gospel. Thus a physical affliction brought to tens of thousands a spiritual blessing.

If success in the service of Christ were to be judged by popularity, then one of the most successful pastors of all time was Paul of Samosata. Yet he achieved his popularity in a most strange way. He banished all singing from his services. And he rarely celebrated the eucharist. The centre of each act of worship was a long sermon, in which he expounded one or two sentences from scripture in great detail. He did not dress in colourful robes, but in a simple black and white cloak – made of the finest material. He sat on a dais facing the congregations. He banished every kind of ornament or decoration from the place of worship, so all eyes focused on him. Indeed that was the true essence of his popularity. On the surface he appeared to want to return to the simplicity of worship, as recorded in scripture. But in truth he was setting himself up as Saviour; and he took away everything that distracted attention from himself. Thus his congregation worshipped him, not Christ; in truth he and Christ were confused in their minds. Many people were attracted by this, because a saviour who is visible and tangible is more appealing than one who can be known only in spirit. But when Paul of Samosata died, there was, of course, no resurrection on earth; so his church died also.

Late in the third century the people of Alexandria rose up against Roman rule. They formed a militia and marched on the governor's palace, taking the governor and all his officers prisoners. Hearing about this rebellion the Emperor in Rome sent his army to lay siege to the city. The Christians in Alexandria found themselves in a terrible dilemma. They were sympathetic with many of the grievances against Roman rule; yet they disapproved of rebellion against legitimate authority as a means of attaining justice. As the siege continued, food in the city became increasingly scarce; and soon many elderly people and young children were dying of starvation. The Bishop of Alexandria, called Anatolius, waited for a night that was pitch dark, with clouds covering the moon and stars. Then with a long rope he climbed over the wall of the city, and ran to the Roman lines. He went to the Roman general and explained that as a Christian he was forbidden from fighting; so he came as a man of peace. He asked permission for the women and children of the city, plus all elderly people, to come out; then the eventual battle could be fought without endangering innocent lives. The general gave his permission; and the following day Anatolius led a great column of people out of the city gates. Afterwards he went back into the city, to offer spiritual comfort to those who remained. He was killed during the final battle, but is recalled with deep gratitude by pagans and Christians alike.

By the seventh and eighth decades of the third century there were large Christian congregations in every city of the empire and in most towns and villages. And in every social class and profession a substantial minority practised the Christian faith. The emperors of the period, while not professing the faith themselves, recognized that for the peace of the empire the Christians should be treated with respect and tolerance. As a result they allowed Christians to build churches in which to worship, many of which exceeded the pagan temples in size and magnificence. But sadly the freedom which Christians now enjoyed began to undermine their character. Many bishops and priests became arrogant and lazy, demanding large sums of money from their people, but doing little work in return; thus the sick were not visited, and new converts were not instructed. Many congregations divided into factions; and although the protagonists claimed that the conflicts were over matters of doctrine, invariably the true cause was power – each faction wanting to rule the church for its own benefit. It is as if the bishops, priests and laity who tarnished the gospel in these ways imagined that God was not watching their wicked actions. Thus when Emperor Diocletian issued decrees ordering a new persecution, some devout Christians believed that Diocletian was being used by God to punish his wayward people.

In his first decree Emperor Diocletian ordered that all church buildings be razed to the ground, and that copies of the scriptures be burnt by fire. In his second decree he ordered that all domestic servants who professed Christianity could be turned into slaves by their masters. Then the Emperor decreed that the leaders of churches should be put into prison, and that every possible means should be used to coerce them into denying their faith. The means of coercion varied from place to place, and person to person. Some leaders were flogged until their flesh was falling from their bones. Some were put on racks and stretched. Others had their skin scraped off, layer by layer, with sharp knives. During these tortures the Christian leaders tried to maintain their courage by singing hymns and psalms at the tops of their voices; their torturers then put rags in their mouths to stop the noise. Some succumbed, and offered sacrifices to the imperial gods. But others kept their faith until the torture caused them to lose consciousness; then they were thrown into pits to die. In a few cases the torturers themselves withdrew from their task before it was complete: they feared that, since Christians were now so numerous, the perpetrators of the persecution might eventually suffer some terrible retribution.

In Nicomedia the soldiers brought an elderly Christian – sadly his name is now forgotten – to the public square. When he refused to deny his faith the governor ordered him to be stripped naked. He was then whipped on every part of his body; but still he maintained his faith. So the soldiers poured vinegar on his wounds. Still he proclaimed his love of Christ. Finally they hoisted him up, and lit a fire beneath him. They slowly roasted each part of his body; and as they did so they constantly demanded that he renounced Christianity. But his last words were a hymn of praise. The stubbornness of this old man spurred the authorities in the city to even greater brutality. They began arresting young women, stripping them naked, and hoisting them up by one leg. These poor women were left dangling, whilst the crowd shouted obscenities at them. Almost invariably the women maintained their faith. The soldiers were then allowed to take them down and violate them; then the women were beheaded. Once the soldiers had rooted out all the young Christian women in the city, they began to search the surrounding villages. But when the young women heard that the soldiers were coming, they jumped into the river and drowned rather than submit to such shameful deeds. Soon the river that runs through Nicomedia was filled with the corpses of beautiful virgins, who have given their lives to Christ.

In the second year of this persecution Emperor Diocletian died. After a time of uncertainty in imperial affairs a man even more evil, Maxentius, assumed power in Rome. Yet under him the persecution took a strange turn. Maxentius had no particular hatred for Christians; indeed he was so absorbed by his own wicked lusts that he hated no one. Rather he saw all his subjects as mere playthings to be exploited for his pleasure. Day by day, and night by night, he ordered both girls and boys to be brought to him; and he corrupted them in the most disgusting ways. He imposed heavy taxes on every household, in order to finance his orgies; and if a man was unable to pay, he was instantly beheaded. He even demanded that newborn babies be brought to him, because he enjoyed slitting them open to examine their entrails. In the face of this terrible brutality the Christians acted as protectors of the common people. Since they had no fear of death, they were willing to risk arrest and execution in order to smuggle the young women and men, the children and the babies, out of the city. Every night brave Christians led groups through the dark alleys and then over the city walls. Some were caught, and suffered torture beyond description. But this did not deter the others; and by their bravery thousands were saved.

After nine years of appalling cruelty, the Emperor contracted a disease which started with severe inflammation of his genitals. His genitals then became ulcerous, and the ulcers spread into his intestines. Soon his intestines had become a teeming mass of worms, which began to eat the great layers of fat which his body had acquired through over-indulgence. The stench which emanated from him was so great that doctors could not get near him without vomiting. As he wrestled with this terrible sickness, he was filled with remorse for his cruelty. And he came to believe that the sickness was an act of revenge by the Christian God. Thus he issued a decree which stopped all persecution of Christians, and restored to them the sites where their churches had stood. He concluded his decree by demanding that the Christians, in response to his clemency, pray to their God for his disease to be cured. Almost as soon as this decree was published the disease disappeared; soon afterward, however, the Emperor's heart stopped beating, exhausted by a lifetime of depravity. In the meantime Maximin, the commander of the eastern region of the empire, refused to accept the decree, and continued to persecute Christians in Asia. And when he heard that the Emperor had died, he seized power.

Thus, under the tyrant Maximin, a new wave of persecution swept through the empire – which was, God be praised, the final wave. Maximin was aware that Christians were now very numerous in every part of the empire; indeed in many places they were in a majority. Therefore he needed the full-hearted support of every pagan. To win this support he forged a memorandum from Pilate, the governor of Palestine under whom our Saviour was crucified. In this forgery Pilate brings many charges against Christ and his followers, including incest and cannibalism, and purports to offer evidence in support of these charges. In addition Maximin's officers found a number of people who had once been Christians, but had turned their backs on the faith; and these people were persuaded to sign statements claiming that incest and cannibalism still persist in the churches. By these foul means Maximin cloaked his cruelty in the robes of justice and peace. Maximin also presented himself as a deeply religious man, filled with zeal to restore the ancient rituals and ceremonies of paganism. To this end he appointed pagan priests in every city and town, and devoted huge sums of money to repairing the old temples. Unlike his predecessor, Maximin did not conduct the torture and execution of Christians in public, since he recognized that this evoked sympathy and admiration for them, and even swelled their ranks. His sole object was to reduce the number of Christians as rapidly as possible, since he perceived them as enemies of his rule and depravity; and he correctly calculated that this could best be achieved with stealth and discretion.

When the winter arrived, the rains that normally come at this season failed; so the people were unable to plant their crops. By the spring grain stored from the previous harvest was running out, and the terrible shadow of famine fell across the empire. At the same time a new disease struck. It took the form of a malignant pustule, which owing to its fiery appearance was known as a carbuncle; this spread across the entire body, but its chief target was the eyes, causing countless thousands to go blind. By the summer the combination of famine and disease was turning healthy people into ghosts of their former selves. By the autumn millions were dying. In this terrible calamity the Christians displayed their true character by going out day and night to tend the sick and bury the dead. In the meantime the Emperor in his wicked folly decided to attack Armenia, on the eastern border of the empire. Greed for the wealth of the Armenians motivated him. The Armenians, most of whom were Christians, had long been staunch allies of Rome; so they were deeply shocked at this unprovoked action. They retaliated with great courage, spurred on by the knowledge that, if they defeated and destroyed this evil Emperor, they would be aiding their Christian brothers and sisters throughout the empire. While they did not succeed in their noble ambition, they left the Emperor and his legions so weakened that God's chosen instrument as the imperial protector of the church could win a great victory.

Constantine, who was the rightful heir to the imperial throne, was prompted by God to rise up against the wicked tyrant who occupied it. He looked with pity at the plight of Christians throughout the empire, and felt he had a divine duty to set them free. Thus he gathered an army and marched into Italy. The people in the northern part of the country welcomed him with unreserved joy, giving his soldiers whatever scraps of food they had. The wicked tyrant was too frightened to march out and confront his adversary. Instead he drew all his soldiers inside the walls of Rome, to await Constantine's arrival. Within a very short time Constantine and his men arrived within sight of the imperial capital, with only the river standing between him and the city walls. The Emperor decided that he must now come out and fight. So he ordered his men to construct a pontoon of boats across the river, with planks spread across the boats; then he marched over the planks with his army. Constantine had in the meantime being praying for victory; and he saw in the sky a giant cross – which assured him of God's strength. Constantine's army was far smaller than the Emperor's, but his men fought with great courage, knowing that their cause was just. The Emperor's soldiers proved as cowardly as the Emperor himself, and soon fled back over the pontoon. But in the scramble over half the Emperor's army found themselves crowded onto the pontoon; and under this weight it collapsed, and most of the soldiers were drowned. Thus Constantine was able to make a new pontoon, and march into Rome without resistance.

Once Constantine had installed himself as emperor, he issued a series of decrees and ordinances relating to religion. Here is the first: 'For a long time we have believed that freedom of worship should not be denied; every person should be permitted to practice religion according to his own inclination and wish. This will help to promote peace and tranquillity throughout our empire, and to lessen the possibility of conflict and rebellion. We therefore command that all people, Christians and non-Christians alike, should be allowed to follow their own faith without hindrance. We further believe that Christianity should have a special place since, through the observance of Christian worship throughout the empire, the God to whom the Christians pray will shower blessings on us all. Thus all persecution of Christians must cease. Once the Christian churches are thriving in every city and town of the empire, then we can extend our tolerance to all religions. This is because the Christian God is not cruel or jealous, but encourages every sincere attempt by men and women to know the truth and to act righteously. From now on religion of every kind, and especially the Christian religion, should enjoy a place of privilege throughout our empire.'

Here is the second decree which the new Emperor Constantine issued concerning religion: 'In the past the places which the Christians built for worship were seized from them. In some cases they were destroyed, and villas were constructed in their stead. In other cases they were converted for other purposes. We believe that the seizing of these places of worship was theft, and was thus both illegal and immoral. In every case they must be handed back freely, without any demand for money; there must be no hesitation. If any persons have received such places as gifts, they must immediately restore them to the Christians. If any persons have purchased such places, they must also restore them to the Christians; and having done so they may appeal to our generosity, to compensate them for their loss. We know that the Christians also owned other properties which they used for charitable purposes such as healing the sick and nursing the dying; and these places were stolen as well. They too must be restored by their present occupants to the Christians, freely and without charge; and those who have purchased them may appeal to our generosity. I emphasize that there must be no delay in setting right this wrong. Those who seized these Christian buildings were stealing from God himself; may God forgive such a terrible crime.'

After some weeks as emperor Constantine addressed the following letter to the bishops of the churches throughout the empire: 'I have received many letters from bishops and priests from churches in every region. I must sadly conclude that there are many quarrels and disputes, splits and divisions amongst Christians. The issues over which Christians disagree are often doctrinal, but also concern authority – who is the rightful leader of a particular congregation and property. This is a matter of deep sadness, and must grieve the God whom Christians worship. I am convinced, however, that amidst these disagreements there is the true Catholic Church, which in matters of doctrine and authority is the true heir of the apostles. It is, therefore, my will and purpose that in all cities and towns of the empire the Catholic Church should be upheld; and that property which had formerly been seized should be returned to the Catholic Church. My hope is that heretical sects who oppose the Catholic Church will abandon their independence, and in humility and repentance return to the Catholic fold. I also decree that the bishops and priests of Catholic congregations should be exempt from all public service, so that they may devote themselves wholly to spiritual and pastoral duties.'

After some months as emperor Constantine addressed the following letter to the bishops of the churches throughout the empire: 'I continue to receive numerous letters from Christian leaders in every region. It is clear to me that many of you have become so inflamed with the spirit of enmity and hatred that you have forgotten your own salvation. Local synods are convened to resolve disagreements and disputes. But in some cases these synods fail to reach any conclusion; in other cases the agreements are ignored and flouted as soon as the synod is over. Your Saviour teaches you to practise unity and concord; but you have become masters of disunity and discord. In this way you bring disgrace on yourselves, and on your most holy religion. I therefore believe that under God I have a duty to impose unity on the church, using the imperial power which God has vested in me to put an end to all disputes. For this purpose I am convening a synod to which all Christian leaders will come. I will preside at this synod, listening to the beliefs and opinions of anyone who wishes to speak. I will then weigh up what I have heard, and issue my judgement. I perform this task with reluctance; I have not sought it, but your misbehaviour has forced it upon me. May the divine power of the great God keep you all in good health, both in spirit and in body, for many years.'

FURTHER READING

J. Stevenson (ed) *A New Eusebius: documents illustrative of the history of the church to AD 337*, London, SPCK 1957.
[Based on the collection edited by B.J. Kidd, SPCK 1920 & 1923]

Eusebius *The History of the Church from Christ to Constantine* translated with an introduction by G.A. Williamson, London, Penguin 1989.